1987

Front cover: Buff Cocker Spaniel

HOWELL

Beginner's guide to

Cocker Spaniels

Yvonne Knapper &
Sheila Zabawa

Editor
Dennis Kelsey-Wood

HOWELL BOOK HOUSE Inc.
230 Park Avenue
New York, N.Y. 10169

Library of Congress Cataloging-in-Publication Data

Knapper, Yvonne.
Howell beginner's guide to cocker spaniels.

Bibliography: p. 43.
Discusses the history, care, training and breeding of cocker spaniels.
1. Cocker spaniels. [1. Cocker spaniels. 2. Dogs]
I. Zabawa, Sheila. II. Title. III. Title: Beginner's guide to cocker spaniels.
SF429.C55K53 636.7'52 87-3421
ISBN 0-87605-915-9

Printed in Hong Kong through Bookbuilders Ltd.

Contents

1. History of the Breed

The Cocker Spaniel, a very popular dog, is the smallest of the gundog breeds. It is an ideal companion, an excellent show dog and also performs well in obedience competitions. In its role as a show dog the Cocker's handsome and abundant coat is much admired; as a companion dog, or if it is to be trained to the gun, its coat may be tailored accordingly.

Origins

The versatile Cocker stems from the same roots as its cousin the English Cocker Spaniel. Both breeds have as their progenitors the Sussex Spaniel and the Field Spaniel, and Spaniels have been known in British canine history since the 14th century. As time went by, and guns took the place of falcons, hunters began to look for different qualities in their sporting dogs and the land Spaniel came to be of greater importance. The terms Springer and Cocker described some of the dogs, the name 'Cocker' being applied to the smallest sporting Spaniels, though this definition was based purely on size and weight.

Cockers are merry, active dogs, but they also know when to relax and enjoy life.

DEVELOPMENT OF BREED TYPES FROM 1880

(artist's impression)

The mid 1850s saw the arousal of interest in dog exhibitions in England, and classes for Cockers were scheduled at a show exclusively for sporting spaniels held at Birmingham in 1859. Later, the classification was dropped in favor of the description large size or small size spaniels; Cockers became eligible for entry in the small size classes with a weight limit of 25 pounds. If a dog weighed more than this it was known as a Field Spaniel. The Field Spaniel has a recorded connection with the Sussex Spaniel when a Sussex sire named Fred was bred to a Field Spaniel named Betty; among their progeny was the Cocker Spaniel Obo, later to become Champion Obo, his breed determined by his weight.

By 1883 classes for Cockers had again been introduced to the show scene and Mr. James Farrow of Ipswich, Suffolk, exhibited Obo, Miss Obo and Sally Obo. The breed was on its way as a show dog as well as a sporting Spaniel, but it was not until 1892 that the English Kennel Club granted separate classification to the Cocker Spaniel. With the Cocker officially recognized as a separate breed it is interesting to note that the dogs were low on the leg and long in body. The present day appearance of the Cocker Spaniel is markedly different, although its weight is similar.

The famous Ch Obo was bred to a bitch called Chloe II; she was exported, in whelp, to her new owner in New Hampshire, USA. From her litter, one dog became Champion Obo II whilst a litter brother was Champion Hornell Silk. Both dogs were solid black, but not dominant black; their pedigrees contained dogs of all the known Spaniel colors which are still seen in the breed today.

Another English dog, Champion Brush, was also much admired on both sides of the Atlantic prior to the popularity of Ch Obo; the subsequent mingling of the Brush and Obo bloodlines proved extremely valuable and produced 80% of the Cocker Spaniel champions in America between 1884 and 1900. Further exports from the Obo line, and others, went to the USA, but it was Ch Obo II which exerted most influence on the breed in those crucial formative years.

Ch Obo II was whelped in 1882 and became a prepotent sire, that is, one which stamps its type on its progeny regardless of the attributes, or lack of them, in its partners. Obo's half sister, Miss Obo II, was also a great producer and passed on her good qualities to her puppies. Dogs and bitches with these breeding qualities are rare, but when such animals exist they usually found a strain. In the case of the Cocker Spaniel, the Obo line seems to have been the foundation of not only a strain, or a breed, but two breeds! Today, Cockers being exhibited anywhere have pedigrees which can be traced back through the Obo line to the Field and Sussex Spaniel connection many generations ago.

In the 1920s a dog named Robinhurst Foreglow sired some excellent offspring. One was Red Brucie, sire of 34 champions culminating with Champion My Own Brucie, twice winner of Best in Show at the Westminster Show in New York — America's premier dog show. These great wins were achieved in 1940 and 1941.

By then the Cocker's overall appearance was changing. It had become a taller dog and was shorter backed. The Cocker was also beginning to carry more coat, and selective breeding in the ensuing years served to establish the heavy coats we know today. As with all changing and developing situations, there was a percentage of those involved who welcomed new ideas and others who resented them. When opinions cannot be reconciled a schism results. There were two different factions in the Cocker Spaniel breed in America, and two types of Cocker Spaniel. In 1945 the American Kennel Club recognized them as separate breeds. The more progressive type of dog retained the name of Cocker Spaniel whilst the more conservative type was designated the English Cocker Spaniel. The latter has retained its popularity in Britain, but in the USA the Cocker takes the lead and was recorded as the most popular of all breeds in 1947, and again in 1983 and 1984, with more than 90,000 annual registrations.

The modern Cocker, a truly made in America model, enjoys worldwide acclaim, with a strong following in Britain, Scandinavia, Europe, Australia, New Zealand, South Africa and South America. Wherever canine exhibition is popular the Cocker Spaniel will be found, and although supreme as a show dog the Cocker is also much sought after as a companion.

Controversy

When the Cocker Spaniel was re-introduced into Britain, via Holland, as a show dog in the 1960s it was designated the Spaniel (American Cocker) by the English Kennel Club. The dog known in America as the English Cocker Spaniel is officially referred to by the English Kennel Club as the Spaniel (Cocker). In the early 1970s the English Kennel Club announced its intention to transfer the Spaniel (American Cocker) from the Gundog Group to the Utility Group, but pressure from the breed fanciers in the UK, and worldwide, was so strong that it was allowed to remain officially in the Gundog Group. In the USA the Cocker Spaniel is classed in the Group known as Sporting.

2. The Selection and Care of a Puppy

Prospective Cocker Spaniel owners should consider their responsibilities towards their dog before deciding this is the breed they wish to own. Cockers need regular exercise, and regular grooming. Pet dogs require professional trimming every 6-8 weeks, and the coat care and trimming of the show dog is important and intricate. Many people enjoy grooming but, if you do not, it would be better to choose another breed. People who live in apartments, or who are away from home for long periods, during which the puppy would be left alone, are not able to provide the freedom and socialization a puppy needs in order to develop into a sensible, friendly, adult companion dog.

Note the excellent head on this Silver puppy

Obtaining a Puppy

It is always preferable to buy your puppy direct from the breeder. You may find breeders' advertisements in your local paper, or you may be able to attend a dog show in your area and contact some breeders there. Visiting a dog show will give you the opportunity to see the full beauty and size of the adult dog, and the opportunity to see the various colors. There may be a Cocker Spaniel breed club in your part of the country; details of such societies may be obtained from your national Kennel Club. A breed club representative may be able to introduce you to a breeder with puppies for sale, and also to provide other useful information. Dog shows are advertised in the various canine press—in which breeders also advertise — so one of these could be ordered from your local newsagent.

Choosing a Puppy

Many breeds have a few health problems which are well known and which should be taken into consideration before purchasing a puppy. The Cocker is no exception; its chief difficulty is that of heritable cataracts. Sincere breeders have their breeding stock examined by veterinarians holding a diploma in ophthalmology who are empowered to issue certificates of freedom from clinical evidence of eye diseases in the dogs they examine. Of course the breeder should show you the eye examination certificates relating to the puppy's parents, and these should, preferably, be dated within 6 months of the puppy's birth. If such documents are not available the answer is simple: go to a breeder who will provide them. This advice applies to the purchase of any Cocker puppy, be it a pet dog, show prospect or future breeding stock.

At the age of 8 weeks a puppy should be fully weaned and ready to go to a new home. At this age it is ready to accept new surroundings with the minimum of difficulties. Older puppies, or adult dogs, take more time to settle. Do not handle a puppy unless the breeder gives permission, and then hold it carefully. The healthy puppy should feel plump and comfortable in your hands, not thin and scared. Puppies should have a healthy covering of fat, but should not be pot bellied as this could indicate the presence of intestinal worms.

Check the puppy's ears; they should be quite clean and have no unpleasant odor. Its teeth should meet in a scissor bite, that is, the top front teeth should close evenly and tightly over the bottom teeth; the puppy's jaws should be even. Mouth defects, if serious, can lead to discomfort for the dog. A puppy's eyes should be bright and intelligent. There should be no signs of any discharge or discomfort and the puppy should appear happy, playful, and interested in what is going on. Puppies should have merry, wagging tails. The pup which tucks its tail between its legs may be shy and nervous. If you are selecting a prospective show puppy be aware that a low set tail is a breed fault, but if you are choosing a pet puppy this is not important unless accompanied by signs of nervousness.

Coat Color and Texture

The Cocker's coat is its crowning glory. Many purchasers have a preference for a particular color, but a sound, healthy pup should be the priority choice. The basic decision should lie between a solid color dog, black, black-and-tan or buff, or the particolors which may be black-and-white, red-and-white or tricolor. Chocolate or chocolate particolors are also favored by some breeders.

The texture of the coat is very important. The Cocker's coat should be flat, silky or slightly wavy, and have an easy care texture. Curly, cottony or woolly coats are incorrect and are much more difficult to groom. A puppy's coat should be clean and there should be no signs of dandruff; there should also be no signs of itching, scratching or sore places on its skin.

A Male or a Female Puppy

Either sex make good companions, but the adult bitch will probably be in heat approximately every 6 months. Your veterinarian can advise you on ways of lessening the difficulty with her cycles, but at such times she must be guarded against the attention of male dogs unless you wish to breed her. Both sexes are good with children and are easy to train, but if you are considering breeding a litter then a good quality female should be your choice.

Temperament

The Cocker's temperament should be friendly, merry and willing to please regardless of its sex. A gundog should show a strong inclination to work. When purchasing your puppy you should note the attitude of its dam; check that she has a friendly, outgoing nature as mothers teach their puppies early lessons in behavior.

Paperwork

When you purchase your puppy be sure you are given a receipt or sales contract. You should also receive the Kennel Club registration papers at the time of purchase though sometimes these are delayed for reasons beyond the breeder's control. In such a case ask for the Kennel Club registration certificate numbers of the sire and the dam to be included in the evidence of sale. You should also receive a copy of the puppy's pedigree showing 4-5 generations of its breeding. Pedigrees are fascinating documents; be sure to keep yours safely.

The breeder should supply you with a detailed diet sheet for the puppy and this should be followed to the letter. Any changes in a puppy's diet should be made gradually, and not during its first few days in its new home.

The Journey Home

When you collect your puppy it is best to take with you a strong carton, one from the supermarket will do, and line it with newspaper and an old towel or a piece of blanket. Let the pup ride home in the box, preferably, held on someone's knee. This will make it feel more secure and less liable to be car sick.

On Arriving Home

The puppy needs a few days to settle into its new surroundings. Remember it is a

Above: Starting young! The first lesson in show posing for this baby pup. It also helps the breeder decide whether the puppy has show potential.

Left: Investigating the flower garden and looking for mischief.

baby and needs undisturbed sleep as well as playtimes. Do not make any changes to its diet yet and take the puppy to your veterinarian as soon as possible for a health check and advice on immunization against the infectious canine diseases.

If your new puppy is reluctant to eat at first give it time to adjust. Check that clean drinking water is always within the puppy's reach, offer food at mealtimes as directed on the diet sheet, but do not offer snacks between meals.

Be sure the puppy has a safe place in your yard to play. If the yard is not completely enclosed and definitely 'puppy proof' as far as escape is concerned make a pen, or run, for the pup so that it cannot get into any trouble, wander or get hurt. Do not leave the puppy outside unsupervised for too long and check that there is shade, or shelter, depending on the climate in which you live.

3. Training

With its gundog background the Cocker Spaniel is a willing worker and responsive to training. In the domestic environment training usually presents no problem but do not expect too much too soon.

The first thing a puppy should learn is its call name. Use it right from the start. Teach your puppy to come to you when you call its name, and praise it for responding. Your dog must answer your call always; it could be a life saver in a moment of danger. Training a puppy is an adult responsibility and is not child's play.

Socialization

Your puppy should not mix with other dogs, nor be walked in a public place where other dogs exercise, until your veterinarian assures you that its immunization program is complete and the pup is fully protected against infection. Then it is safe for your puppy to socialize.

When it is ready to meet the rest of the world bear in mind not only the puppy's small size but its lack of experience, its curiosity or, perhaps, fear of the unknown. Introduce your puppy gradually to the outside world, in safe, quiet surroundings at first; take time to work up to busy, and possibly hazardous situations when it has gained sufficient self-assurance and you are able to understand what its reactions might be under various circumstances. Shocks and frights occurring through an owner's lack of foresight are a setback to secure socialization.

Rewards

All sensible training of dogs is a matter of patience and repetition of simple commands or actions which the dog is able to understand. Praise for correct behavior is far more important than punishment for errors. A dog does not remember the mistake he made an hour ago, or even a few minutes previously. It does remember the praise given for success, however limited that success might be from your point of view.

Rewards are best given in words of praise, pats, hugs and pleased voices; a verbal scolding is more subduing than a slap. Food rewards, candy or cookies are to be deplored; avoid this trap! Such rewards may make the puppy overweight, or they may take the edge off a finicky puppy's appetite and create poor eating habits. Food rewards can also make a dog a food pest, one which expects snacks from your table or cake from visitors. Forbid food rewards from the start; plan your training strategy in advance.

House Training

This part of your puppy's training may overlap several parts of his early education. Patience is needed. Dogs are not naturally dirty creatures. They do not like to foul their own beds, but they definitely need to be taught where they can attend to their own natural functions and be praised for their co-operation.

Most litters of puppies are newspaper trained by their breeders, so in the early stages they will look for newspapers and you should have a stack of them in readiness. However, your puppy will soon learn to respond to being taken out into the yard, or put into an outside run, when it needs to defecate or urinate. Always remove soiled papers and clean up the run if the puppy has fouled it. This will keep you busy for young puppies having four meals a day will naturally have frequent bowel movements and will urinate often. Puppies need to 'go' after they have been fed, when they wake up from a nap, and almost any time! If the pup looks distressed take it outside right away. By anticipating your pup's toilet needs you can considerably shorten the housebreaking period. Should the older puppy still not be clean and dry overnight the crate training method may be tried; it usually works.

It is very useful to have a travel crate for your Cocker; a wire mesh or fibreglass crate measuring not less than 45x60 cm (18x24 in) is recommended. It makes car trips safer, and in the home many pups like to be fed in their crates so they can eat undisturbed. The crate becomes their den, or refuge, and if they are put to bed in it last thing at night, after a toilet trip outside, and let out early in the morning then overnight training is often accomplished rapidly. This is for the older puppy, of course; the very young simply have not developed bowel or bladder control and just cannot wait. Remember, too, that although the dog likes its crate it should not be confined for long periods just to suit your convenience.

Apart from reasons of hygiene, it is important that your puppy's exercise area is kept scrupulously clean so that the habit of coprophagy, that is when a dog eats its own feces, does not develop. This unpleasant problem is sometimes an attempt to keep its own quarters clean, but occasionally a dietary deficiency may be indicated. It is thought that a vitamin B supplement, brewer's yeast for example, may be useful in such cases, but removing all temptation is the best preventative.

Leash Training

A puppy should be introduced to its collar and leash in its own backyard. Cockers do not usually resist leash training though they may consider it a silly game at first.

The collar should not be too tight, but neither should it be loose enough to slip over the puppy's head. Let the pup become accustomed to the collar before attaching a leash. When the leash is clipped to the collar let it dangle free at first, then take hold of it while still allowing the puppy to go where it pleases. Gradually teach the puppy to walk where you want it to and of course, reward its good efforts.

Early leash training lessons should last for only a few minutes; increase the time as co-operation is acquired. When the puppy really catches on to the idea let it try its (your?) skills in a quiet street where the sidewalk is not crowded. Once the puppy is used to this widen its experience to busier neighborhoods, parks, and playgrounds where dogs are permitted.

Noise

Undue noise is usually the reason why neighbors complain. A dog which barks continually in the yard, or barks and whines in the house when the owners are out, can be very annoying indeed. Train your pup to remain on its own for short periods right from the start. Leave the pup when it has settled after a meal; go to the store or do a similar errand which does not take too long. When the puppy has become used to your short absences gradually extend the time. Provide suitable, non-toxic, harmless toys for your puppy to play with. It is usually the bored and lonely puppy which whines and barks unnecessarily; dogs are expected to bark at the approach of unrecognized visitors or intruders.

Consideration for your Dog

Dogs, like most animals, appreciate a regular routine. That is how they learn.

From the time your puppy joins the family be firm, be fair, be forgiving. Start as you mean to go on. Letting a baby pup sleep on your bed and later deciding it must sleep elsewhere will not be understood by the dog. Allowing a puppy to play with an old slipper or glove and then punishing it for chewing your new shoes or best gloves is not fair to either of you. Buy the pup safe toys from the pet store.

At all times be observant. Note any unusual behavior in your puppy, any little physical signs of distress. They may be an early warning that something is wrong, and if a health problem develops it will assist your veterinarian if you can present a comprehensive case history.

Consideration for your Family

Cockers love to be part of family life and many live well into their teens. A well trained dog should give you years of pleasure and interest, and be appreciated by all the family. A dog is inquisitve and likes to investigate every inch of its territory. If you do not want paw prints all over your house decide which rooms are off limits and keep doors closed. You may have to train your family to do this as your Cocker cannot be expected to understand that it should not enter a room if the door is open, but it certainly understands one that is shut.

Legal Responsibilities

Be aware of your legal responsibilities as a dog owner. These may vary from country to country and from state to state. For its own protection your dog should wear a collar with an identification tag attached showing your telephone number. Check whether you are required to buy a dog license. Are you required to carry insurance for your dog? If this is not a legal requirement it could still be advantageous to do so. Dogs can cause damage to persons and property; they can cause accidents for which you might be held liable. Be sure that you know the legal obligations which apply to dog owners in your own area and obey the law.

4. Adult Management

Your Cocker's basic training should have been accomplished by the time it reaches adulthood but there will still be some extra things for the dog, and you, to learn. For example, some dogs will never like fireworks, thunderstorms, heavy traffic or busy shopping centers. They have exceptionally acute hearing and probably are more sensitive to vibrations than we are. We should show understanding of reasonable fear and stress.

The family pet, and the show dog too, will enjoy travelling in the car. The travel crate makes life easier, and safer for all, but remember your Cocker needs its comfort stops too. Carry fresh drinking water and a bowl, and be sure the dog does not become overheated. Never leave it alone in a parked car in hot weather, or at any time when the sun is on the vehicle.

At vacation time you may wish to leave your dog in a good boarding kennel. If so, check well in advance by visiting local boarding establishments and choosing one which you can see is well run, and which is recommended by other clients. Never leave this decision until the last minute.

Buff Cocker Spaniel

Nutrition

By the age of 6 months a puppy's 4 meals per day schedule should have reduced to 2 — a light breakfast and an evening meal. Some dogs stick to this regime for life; others progress to 1 meal a day. The actual time of the meal does not matter but it is desirable that it should be the same time every day. After feeding, the dog should be let out for a short toilet trip and then allowed to rest undisturbed to digest its meal.

There are so many excellent commercial dog foods that it is usually only a matter of choosing a brand which is easily available and which the dog likes. So much research has been done in animal nutrition, and the dog's food needs are now so well understood, that commercially manufactured diets are far better balanced than many home recipes. The important point is to read the instructions for feeding printed on every can or pack of food, and to follow the directions carefully.

It is also important to choose one particular method of feeding, that is, to use either a canned food diet, or a complete dry food to which water may be added if desired, and to serve it in accordance with the instructions given by the manufacturer. Clean drinking water should always be available for your dog. Some dogs like milk; if so there is no harm in giving this to them. Other dogs cannot tolerate milk at all and will come to no harm through having none.

As a rough guide, a Cocker weighing 11 kg (24 lb) should require about 250 gm (8 oz) of food daily. This may vary according to your particular dog's needs and to the type of food being used. Weigh your dog and calculate the amount it should be fed. Always bear in mind that some Cockers are greedy and will eat everything and look for more, while others may have a more dainty appetite. The amounts of food suggested above are for the maintenance diet of a healthy adult Cocker. A very active dog may need more; an inactive dog will need less. The healthy dog should be neither too fat nor too thin. Of course, pregnant and lactating bitches have different food requirements and these are discussed in chapter 7.

The Obese Cocker

Try to prevent obesity in your dog by discouraging snacks, food rewards and overeating. Resist those pleading Cocker eyes! Should your dog's weight need to be reduced consult your veterinarian. The weight problem could be caused by a hormone imbalance or other illness needing specific treatment. In any case the veterinarian will advise you on commercially prepared obesity diets, or suggest a home recipe. Slimming diets for dogs need to be carefully supervised.

Bones

Large beef marrow bones are ideal teeth cleaners for dogs and should be provided occasionally. Smaller bones, cooked bones, or chicken and chop bones should never be given to your dog. They are dangerous. In lieu of these very hard biscuits, and crunchy dry kibble, are the next best things for healthy teeth and gums. However, if your dog has a weight problem nylon bones from the pet store may be substituted for hard biscuits.

Exercise

Some Cockers take plenty of exercise playing in the yard. Others tend to be lazy. All benefit from regular walks with their owners. The pet Cocker with a well trimmed coat should not present too many grooming problems in bad weather, but the show dog in full coat may need to be supervised more carefully in very wet or snowy conditions. Wet dogs should be dried thoroughly after exercise. There is no set amount of exercise recommended and the Cocker is happy to go along with your ideas on the subject. The only restriction is that dogs under the age of 6 months should never be over exercised.

The Older Cocker

The ageing dog slows down in most respects, and should be allowed to do so. A regular health check is advisable, and its 'booster' shots should be kept up to date. Such dogs may prefer two smaller meals per day and it is important to note whether it drinks more water than usual. If this happens consult your veterinarian for advice. Also note whether the senior citizen dog is coughing, and that its teeth, gums and ears are healthy and clean. After its bath be sure to dry the dog thoroughly, or remind your canine beautician of the dog's advanced age. Remember the Cocker loves to look nice and to remain an active, important member of the family all its life.

Gold Cocker Spaniel

5. Coat Care and Trimming

Bathing, grooming and trimming are important features of a Cocker Spaniel's life, not only for health and beauty reasons but because regular coat care involves close contact between dog and owner and helps build a bond of love between them. Show dogs are prepared for exhibition by their owners or handlers who attend to all the details in expert fashion. Many pet owners also become competent trimmers, but others prefer to make a regular appointment with a professional canine beautician. In this case the owner will still need to groom the dog thoroughly between appointments. A neglected coat becomes matted and uncomfortable for the dog; knots and tangles can harbor parasites, conceal scratches and sore places which, if unnoticed, may lead to bigger problems.

A professional grooming table makes coat care much easier.

Grooming Equipment

Pet owners, exhibitors, breeders and professional groomers need the same brushes and combs for their Cockers, and those who bathe and trim their own dogs need other items too. The following is a comprehensive list:

Coarse comb with widely spaced teeth.
Fine comb (sometimes called a flea comb).
Nylon and bristle hair brush.
A pure bristle brush is also a good investment.
Slicker brush.
Hairdressing shears.
Fine thinning shears, teeth on one blade only.
Electric clipper, e.g. Oster A5 with No. 10 blade.
Electric hair dryer, preferably a floor standing model.
Nail clipper, guillotine type.
Tooth scaler.
Steady grooming table with non-slip surface.

Most beginners build up their grooming equipment gradually, perhaps buying some of it second hand. If you do not have a separate grooming room choose a place where a scattering of dog hair is not going to bother the rest of the family. If you do not have a dog tub then the kitchen sink will do. Whatever the bath, always use a rubber mat so the dog does not slip, use a shower spray and do not let the dog stand in water. Plenty of old towels are essential for blotting most of the moisture from the dog's coat before the blow drying begins.

Another necessary item is a good shampoo. There are many of these formulated for dogs, but those made for humans are equally satisfactory. Whatever the choice, the shampoo should be mild and non-irritating. Do not use medicated, anti-dandruff or treatment shampoos without veterinary advice, and then only according to instructions. Some dogs, like some humans, are allergic to certain chemicals which may cause a skin reaction.

Grooming Technique

Provided it is done on a regular basis grooming sessions should not take too long. Start when the pup is quite young, before its coat has grown long and heavy. Teach it to lie on the grooming table in the following manner: with its head to your left take hold of its outside legs and gently pull the dog towards you so that from the standing position it comes easily to lying on one side. Dogs quickly become accustomed to this and relax and enjoy grooming sessions; so does the owner who does not have to struggle with a wriggling dog!

The slicker brush, which has hooked pins, may be used on the pet dog, but this brush should only be used with caution on the show dog's coat as it may be too harsh and tear the hair you wish to preserve. Be sure to groom both sides of the dog down to the skin, paying particular attention to the underside, to the point where the legs join the body and to the ear feathering. There must be no tangles left and it should be possible to run a comb completely through the coat. Many new owners make the mistake of brushing only the top layer of hair leaving a

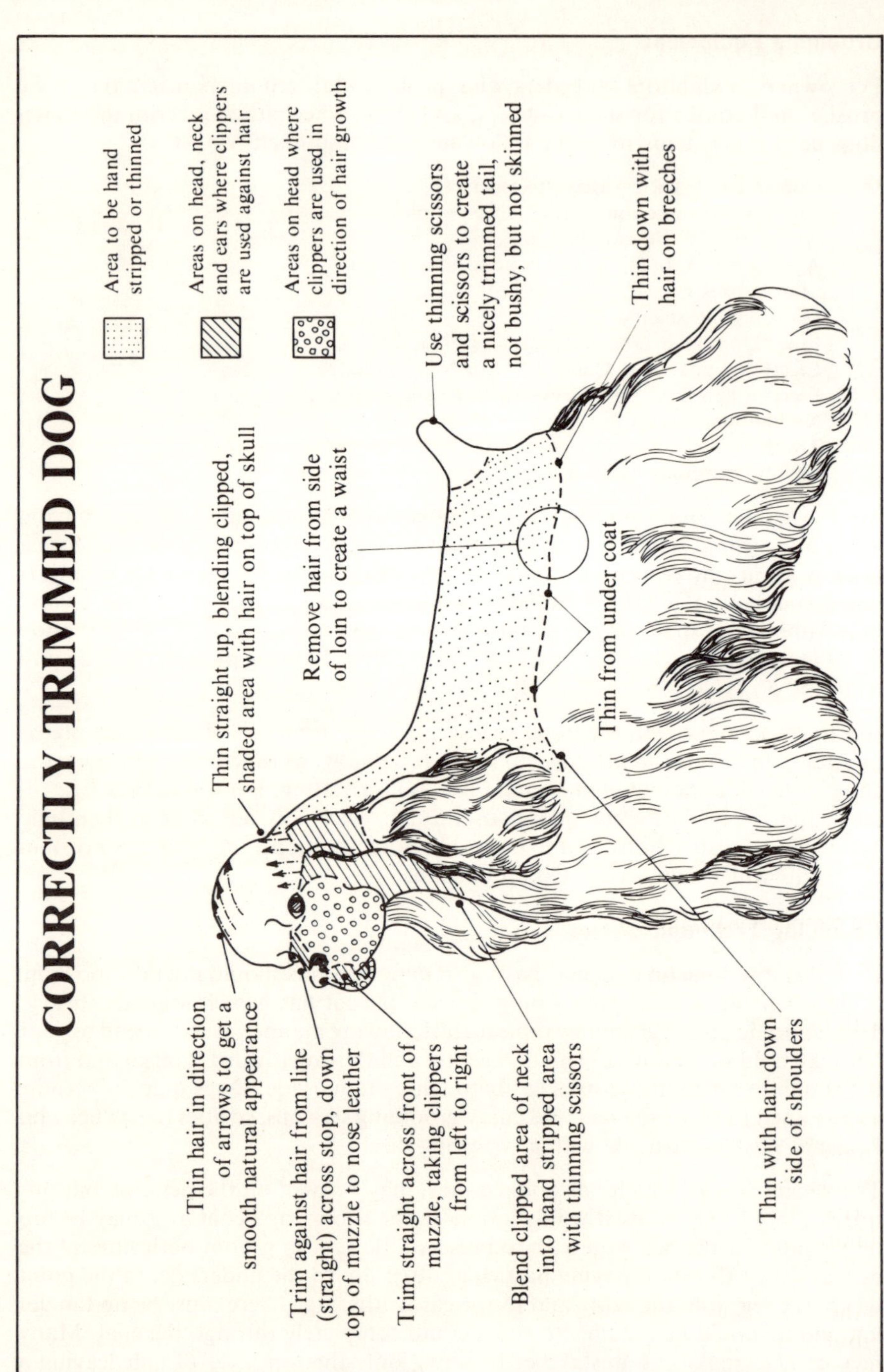

CORRECTLY TRIMMED DOG
Area to be hand stripped or thinned
Areas on head, neck and ears where clippers are used against hair
Areas on head where clippers are used in direction of hair growth
Thin hair in direction of arrows to get a smooth natural appearance
Thin straight up, blending clipped, shaded area with hair on top of skull
Remove hair from side of loin to create a waist
Use thinning scissors and scissors to create a nicely trimmed tail, not bushy, but not skinned
Thin down with hair on breeches
Thin from under coat
Trim against hair from line (straight) across stop, down top of muzzle to nose leather
Trim straight across front of muzzle, taking clippers from left to right
Blend clipped area of neck into hand stripped area with thinning scissors
Thin with hair down side of shoulders

blanket of matted fur underneath. Guard against this error as it could mean that the dog's coat would have to be shaved off completely in a severe case.

Trimming and Bathing Routine

Many exhibitors prefer to hand strip the Cocker's back coat. If this is your choice, the hand stripping should be done before the dog is bathed as the dead hair is then easier to remove. It may take a long time to master the art, but if you persevere it is well worth the effort as hand stripping produces the most beautiful and long lasting effect. If you have difficulty in gripping the hair with the thumb and forefinger cut two fingers off a strong household glove, the sort that have roughened fingertips, and wear one on the thumb and the other on the index finger; it makes the job much easier, but even so hand stripping cannot be accomplished in one attempt. It may take several sessions over a period of days to complete the task. As each small patch is pulled use the fine comb to remove the loose hair.

Another job which may be done before the dog is bathed is the rough trimming of the head. Using the Oster A5 clipper with a No. 10 blade, or an equivalent machine, start by trimming the upper one third of each ear, inside and out, clipping against the growth of the hair. Do not curve the clipper over the skull, just trim the actual ear.

Stand the dog facing you and run your hand down under its chin until you find the breast bone. Clip upwards, against the hair, from the breast bone to the lower lip, and from the breast bone to the base of each ear forming a clean 'V'.

Looking at the head sideways clip the hair in an upwards direction towards a line between the corner of the eye and the ear. Again, do not allow your clipper to curve over the skull; just clip off any overhanging hair. Clip against the hair under the eyes remembering that the Cocker is not clipped above the eyes. Clip against the hair from the stop, or forehead, to the tip of the nose. Make sure these areas are clipped clean and close.

Be sure to clip tidily around the dog's lower lip but leave the muzzle till last. This area should look plushy and therefore should not be trimmed against the hair but with the growth. The head should look natural and not over barbered. Do not clip the hair out between the eyes as it tends to give a hard expression whereas it should always be soft and appealing.

The Cocker's skull should resemble a hemisphere and the most natural look is attained by carefully handstripping the longer hairs and finishing with the thinning shears which may be used to thin under the hair if it is bushy, or on the surface over the occiput to give a smooth look. Never cut across the hair with the thinning shears; this will leave ugly ridges. Always aim for the smooth look, and comb through to remove loose hair as you thin.

If the dog was not bathed before the head trimming now is the time to put it in the tub. Have the shampoo already prepared in a dispenser bottle, and also a creme rinse if you intend to use one; do not forget the towels. Wet the dog thoroughly with the shampoo spray but keep the water out of its eyes and ears. Apply the prepared shampoo and squeeze the suds through the coat, flushing out all the dirt. Rinse carefully with tepid water and repeat the process. After the second sudsing the Cocker's coat should be rinsed squeaky clean before any conditioning rinse is applied. Finally, squeeze as much moisture as possible from the coat, wrap the dog in dry towels to blot up yet more moisture, but be sure not to rub the coat as this will induce tangling. The dog is then ready to be blow dried with the hairdryer.

Place the dog on your grooming table as for regular brushing but groom the coat as the hot air blows it dry. Begin with the ears, as the feathering takes a long time to dry thoroughly, and then continue in your usual grooming routine until the dog is completely dry all over, and brushed free of all tangles.

If there is still some fine trimming to do on the dog's head attend to that first and check for any stray hairs around the lips. Then take the fine thinning shears and, beginning at the occiput, thin with the hair down the neck towards the withers. Just a few cuts at a time and then comb through with the fine comb; look carefully at the result before you continue — you are aiming for a smooth, natural effect. Thin to the point of the shoulder on each side. When the dog is facing you it should show a clean, straight line from the shoulders to the legs.

To thin from the withers to the tail, including the sides, proceed as follows: thin from underneath the coat, never cutting across the coat remember, a few strokes at a time. Thin and comb. The side coat should blend neatly from the thinned, or hand stripped, back coat and not show ridges. Thin over the loin to create a 'waistline' and emphasize the ribcage.

The Cocker's tail, which should be carried on a straight line with its back, should be thinned neatly, but not so severely that it resembles a carrot. Thin the anal area under the tail and blend in with the breeches and leg coat.

Trimming the feet is most important; it can make or break a dog. With the Cocker standing firmly on all four feet run the hand around one leg and down towards the foot. Keeping a tight hold round the bone lift the dog's foot and trim off the hair around it. Put the foot down, comb the hair round the foot and neaten any stray hairs. Repeat the procedure so that all four feet are neatly trimmed and the back feet blend with the leg coat. Always clean out the hair between the pads; sweat, rubble, stones and similar accumulate there and make it most uncomfortable for the dog to walk.

Check your dog's nails. If they are too long they will spoil the dog's movement. To cut the nails use a guillotine nail clipper and just cut the point off each nail being careful not to cut the quick. Keep some Kwikstop or permanganate of potash crystals handy at nail clipping time just in case a nail bleeds. Black nails are the most difficult to cut as the quick cannot be seen.

Check your dog's teeth as part of the bathing and trimming routine. They should be sparkling clean. Brush the dog's teeth with an ordinary tooth brush; using a smoker's toothpaste will help to remove stains. If the dog's teeth become badly encrusted with tartar the cleaning job is best done by your veterinarian. A tooth

A properly trimmed and groomed Cocker, free from knots and tangles is a comfortable, happy and healthy dog.

scaler may be useful but ask your veterinarian to show you how to use it. Check that your dog's ears are clean and dry. They should not have any unpleasant odor and it is a good plan to keep a bottle of ear cleaning lotion handy to wipe away wax deposits. Routine cleaning of ears and teeth help to prevent trouble developing.

A regular bathing and trimming schedule will keep your pet looking its best and efficient grooming will give the show dog its best chances in the ring. Poor, or neglected, trimming could cost the exhibitor a higher placing at a show, or no ribbons at all!

6. Exhibiting and the Standard of the Breed

The thought of showing dogs appeals more to some people than others. Successful exhibiting needs a competitive nature and a creative talent; it also requires dedication and patience, and the ability to accept failure with good grace and success with modesty. It can be a compelling occupation, and a great challenge. The show dog must be physically fit and presented in perfect coat condition.

The Show Scene

Attend some dog shows before becoming an exhibitor yourself. Watch Cockers being judged and observe the general procedure. The puppy which has been well socialized usually takes to the show ring easily and if you have a local canine society enquire whether there is a ringcraft class which you can attend to boost your confidence. You, and your dog, need to practice walking together as required in the show ring, and you will want to become adept at standing, or stacking, your dog for the judge to see it at its best. The dog also needs to become accustomed to the manner in which a judge examines a dog in the ring.

The Show System

There are different types of shows in each country, and different regulations laid down by the individual Kennel Clubs governing canine exhibition. Each show may add certain general rules of its own and in each case it is the exhibitor's duty to be aware of all rules and regulations and abide by them on pain of disqualification.

In the American show system the dogs compete for points towards a champion's title. They must accumulate 15 points, including two majors (three points or more at one show) in order to become a champion. The number of points awarded at a show can vary according to the number of dogs of each sex competing on the day.

In Britain a dog has to win three challenge certificates (CCs) under three different judges, one CC having been awarded after the dog is a year old, in order to qualify for the title of Show Champion. The full title of champion is only granted by the Kennel Club if the dog has also qualified in Field Trails. At the time of writing only two Cockers have become full champions in the UK.

Exhibitors and breeders should familiarize themselves with the official Kennel Club Standard of the Breed and refer to it regularly. Each standard is based on that issued by the Amercian Kennel Club, though there may be slight differences

SKELETON OF THE AMERICAN COCKER SPANIEL

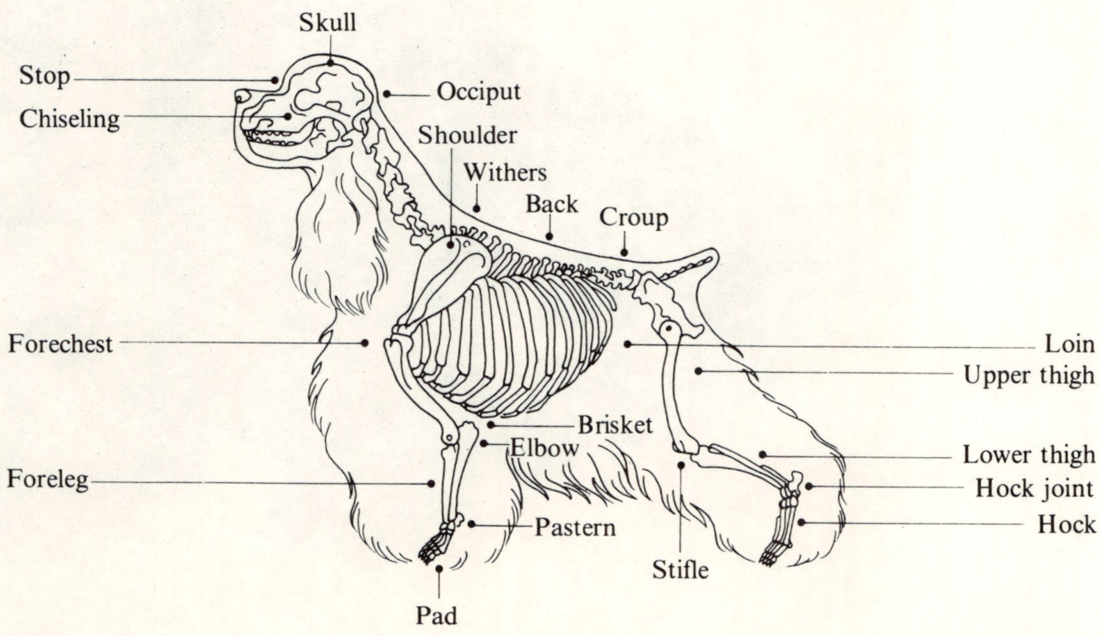

in the wording and certain alterations according to, the policy of the Kennel Club concerned.

An example of the above is that the English Kennel Club does not list any disqualifications but simply states that listed faults shall be penalized, and, in common with other European countries, uses metric measurements. The English Standard also includes an additional note, common to all breeds, that male animals should have two apparently normal testicles fully descended into the scrotum. Failure on this point incurs a penalty only.

Black Cocker Spaniel

Official Standard for the Cocker Spaniel

(Reproduced by kind permission of the American Kennel Club)

General Appearance The Cocker Spaniel is the smallest member of the Sporting Group. He has a sturdy, compact body and a cleanly chiseled and refined head, with the overall dog in complete balance and of ideal size. He stands well up at the shoulder on straight forelegs with a topline sloping slightly toward strong, muscular quarters. He is a dog capable of considerable speed, combined with great endurance. Above all he must be free and merry, sound, well balanced throughout, and in action show a keen inclination to work; equable in temperament with no suggestion of timidity.

Head To attain a well-proportioned head, which must be in balance with the rest of the dog, it embodies the following:
Skull Rounded but not exaggerated with no tendency toward flatness; the eyebrows are clearly defined with a pronounced stop. The bony structure beneath the eyes is well chiseled with no prominence in the cheeks.
Muzzle Broad and deep, with square, even jaws. The upper lip is full and of sufficient depth to cover the lower jaw. To be in correct balance, the distance from the stop to the tip of the nose is one half the distance from the stop up over the crown to the base of the skull.
Teeth Strong and sound, not too small, and meet in a scissors bite.
Nose Of sufficient size to balance the muzzle and foreface, with well-developed nostrils typical of a sporting dog. It is black in color in the blacks and black and tans. In other colors it may be brown, liver or black, the darker the better. The color of the nose harmonizes with the color of the eye rim.
Eyes Eyeballs are round and full and look directly forward. The shape of the eye rims gives a slightly almond-shaped appearance; the eye is not weak or goggled. The color of the iris is dark brown and in general the darker the better. The expression is intelligent, alert, soft and appealing.
Ears Lobular, long, of fine leather, well feathered, and placed no higher than a line to the lower part of the eye.
Neck and Shoulders The neck is sufficiently long to allow the nose to reach the ground easily, muscular and free from pendulous "throatiness." It rises strongly from the shoulders and arches slightly as it tapers to join the head. The shoulders are well laid back forming an angle with the upper arm of approximately 90 degrees which permits the dog to move his forelegs in an easy manner with considerable forward reach. Shoulders are clean-cut and sloping without protrusion and so set that the upper points of the withers are at an angle which permits a wide spring of rib.

Body The body is short, compact and firmly knit together, giving an impression of strength. The distance from the highest point of the shoulder blades to the ground is fifteen (15%) per cent or approximately two inches (10 cm) more than the length from this point to the set-on of the tail. Back is strong and sloping evenly and slightly downward from the shoulders to the set-on of the docked tail. Hips are wide and quarters well rounded and muscular. The chest is deep, its lowest point no higher than the elbows, its front sufficiently wide for adequate heart and lung space, yet not so wide as to interfere with the straightforward movement of the forelegs. Ribs are deep and well sprung. The Cocker Spaniel never appears long and low.
Tail The docked tail is set on and carried on a line with the topline of the back, or slightly higher; never straight up like a terrier and never so low as to indicate timidity. When the dog is in motion the tail action is merry.

HEAD EVALUATION

Correctly proportioned head

Muzzle too long and snipey
Plain stop
Too wide in skull for width of muzzle
Ears set too high
Eyes too small
Skull too flat - no rounding

Over-done, coarse head
Throaty
Loose, drooping eye

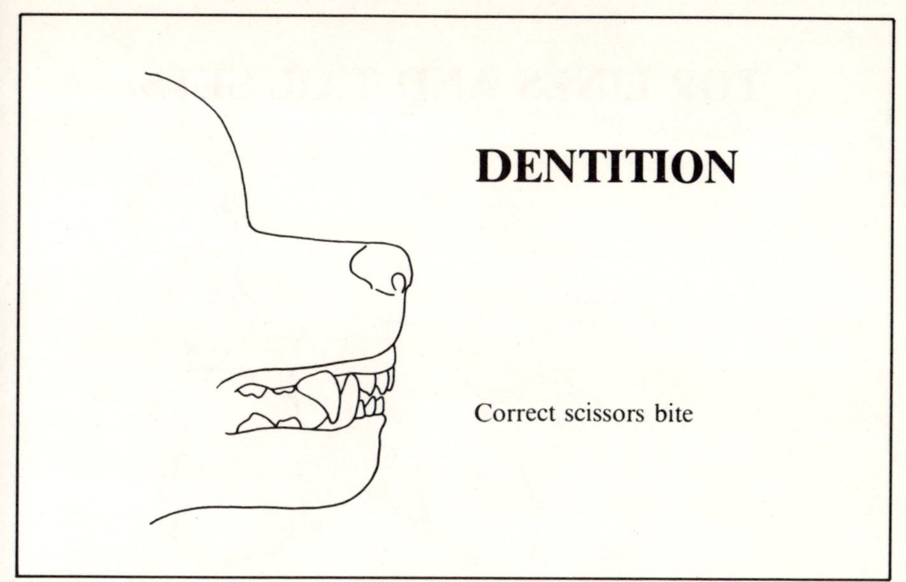

Correct scissors bite

Legs and Feet Forelegs are parallel, straight, strongly boned and muscular and set close to the body well under the scapulae. When viewed from the side with the forelegs vertical, the elbow is directly below the highest point of the shoulder blade. The pasterns are short and strong. The hind legs are strongly boned and muscled with good angulation at the stifle and powerful, clearly defined thighs. The stifle joint is strong and there is no slippage of it in motion or when standing. The hocks are strong, well let down, and when viewed from behind, the hind legs are parallel when in motion and at rest.
Feet Compact, large, round and firm with horny pads; they turn neither in nor out. Dewclaws on hind legs and forelegs may be removed.
Coat On the head, short and fine; on the body, medium length, with enough undercoating to give protection. The ears, chest, abdomen and legs are well feathered, but not so excessively as to hide the Cocker Spaniel's true lines and movement or affect his appearance and function as a sporting dog. The *texture* is most important. The coat is silky, flat or slightly wavy, and of a texture which permits easy care. Excessive or curly or cottony textured coat is to be penalized.

Color and Markings
Black Variety Solid color black, to include black with tan points. The black should be jet; shadings of brown or liver in the sheen of the coat is not desirable. A small amount of white on the chest and/or throat is allowed, white in any other location shall disqualify.
Any Solid Color Other Than Black Any solid color other than black and any such color with tan points. The color shall be of a uniform shade, but lighter coloring of the feather is permissible. A small amount of white on the chest and/or throat is allowed, white in any other location shall disqualify.
Parti-Color Variety Two or more definite, well-broken colors, one of which must be white, including those with tan points; it is preferable that the tan markings be located in the same pattern as for the tan points in the Black and ASCOB varieties. Roans are classified as parti-colors, and may be of any of the usual roaning patterns. Primary color which is ninety percent (90%) or more shall disqualify.

TOP LINES AND TAIL SETS

Tan Points The color of the tan may be from the lightest cream to the darkest red color and should be restricted to ten percent (10%) or less of the color of the specimen; tan markings in excess of that amount shall disqualify.
In the case of tan points in the Black or ASCOB variety, the markings shall be located as follows:
(1) A clear tan spot over each eye
(2) On the sides of the muzzle and on the cheeks
(3) On the undersides of the ears
(4) On all feet and all legs
(5) Under the tail
(6) On the chest (optional, presence or absence not penalized)
Tan markings which are not readily visible or which amount only to traces, shall be penalized. Tan on the muzzle which extends upward, over and joins shall also be penalized. The absence of tan markings in the Black or ASCOB variety in any of the specified locations in an otherwise tan-pointed dog shall disqualify.
Movement The Cocker Spaniel, though the smallest of the sporting dogs, possesses a typical sporting dog gait. Prerequisite to good movement is balance between the front and rear assemblies. He drives with his strong, powerful rear quarters and is properly constructed in the shoulders and forelegs so that he can reach forward without constriction in a full stride to counterbalance the driving force from the rear. Above all, his gait is coordinated, smooth and effortless. The dog must cover ground with his action and excessive animation should never be mistaken for proper gait.
Height The ideal height at the withers for an adult dog is 15 inches (38 cm) and for an adult bitch 14 inches (35 cm). Height may vary one-half inch above or below this ideal. A dog whose height exceeds 15½ inches (39 cm) or a bitch whose height exceeds 14½ inches (37 cm) shall be disqualified. An adult dog whose height is less than 14½ inches (37 cm) or an adult bitch whose height is less than 13½ inches (34 cm) shall be penalized.
Note: Height is determined by a line perpendicular to the ground from the top of the shoulder blades, the dog standing naturally with its forelegs and the lower hind legs parallel to the line of measurement.
Editor's Note: The metric equivalents given in the above do not form part of the official AKC standard and are given for the benefit of readers in countries using metric measurements.

DISQUALIFICATIONS

Color and Markings
Black Variety White markings except on chest and throat.
Any Solid Color Other Than Black Variety White markings except on chest and throat.
Parti-Color Variety Primary color ninety percent (90%) or more.
Tan Points (1) Tan markings in excess of ten percent (10%); (2) Absence of tan markings in black or ASCOB variety in any of the specified locations in an otherwise tan pointed dog.
Height Males over 15½ inches (39 cm); females over 14½ inches (37 cm).

Approved May 10, 1983

7. Breeding

Breeding dogs is a challenge, and the breeder's aim should be to produce puppies which are an improvement on their parents. Breeding should not be undertaken for any other reason.

It is not necessary for a bitch to have puppies for the sake of her health, neither is having a litter likely to be financially profitable for the beginner. The breeding of pet bitches by inexperienced owners may also lead to the perpetuation of serious faults which breeders are trying to eliminate.

Principles of Breeding

The serious breeder undertakes a time consuming, demanding and expensive occupation and a basic understanding of genetics is advantageous. As in all living things some characteristics are controlled by dominant genes; for example, some black Cockers are dominant for that color and can produce none other regardless of the color of their mate. Other characteristics, certain colors and probably some hereditary diseases, may be controlled by recessive genes which only make their presence known when each partner displays, or carries, the recessive factor. The recessive gene can remain hidden for several generations and then, for better or for worse, make its presence known, often as a complete surprise. Genes are responsible for both good and bad points and even the most experienced person sometimes breeds a disappointing litter. This is reducing a vast subject to its most basic form, but once a breeder becomes interested in genetics it can become a fascinating lifetime study.

Breeding Stock

Do your best to avoid the breed's major inherited problems before embarking on a breeding program. The Cocker's worst enemies are eye abnormalities; do not breed from affected animals. Other Cockers which should be excused from any breeding program are those which have had demodectic mange, or bitches which have previously produced puppies having demodectic mange. This skin disease can affect a dog's immune system.

Breeding stock should receive regular 'booster' shots against the infectious canine diseases and regular treatment for intestinal parasites. Unfortunately, the female usually passes *Toxacara canis* (roundworms) to her unborn puppies. *Toxacara canis* is known to be dangerous to children who might come in contact with the eggs which are shed in feces, and a few cases of blindness in such children have been recorded.

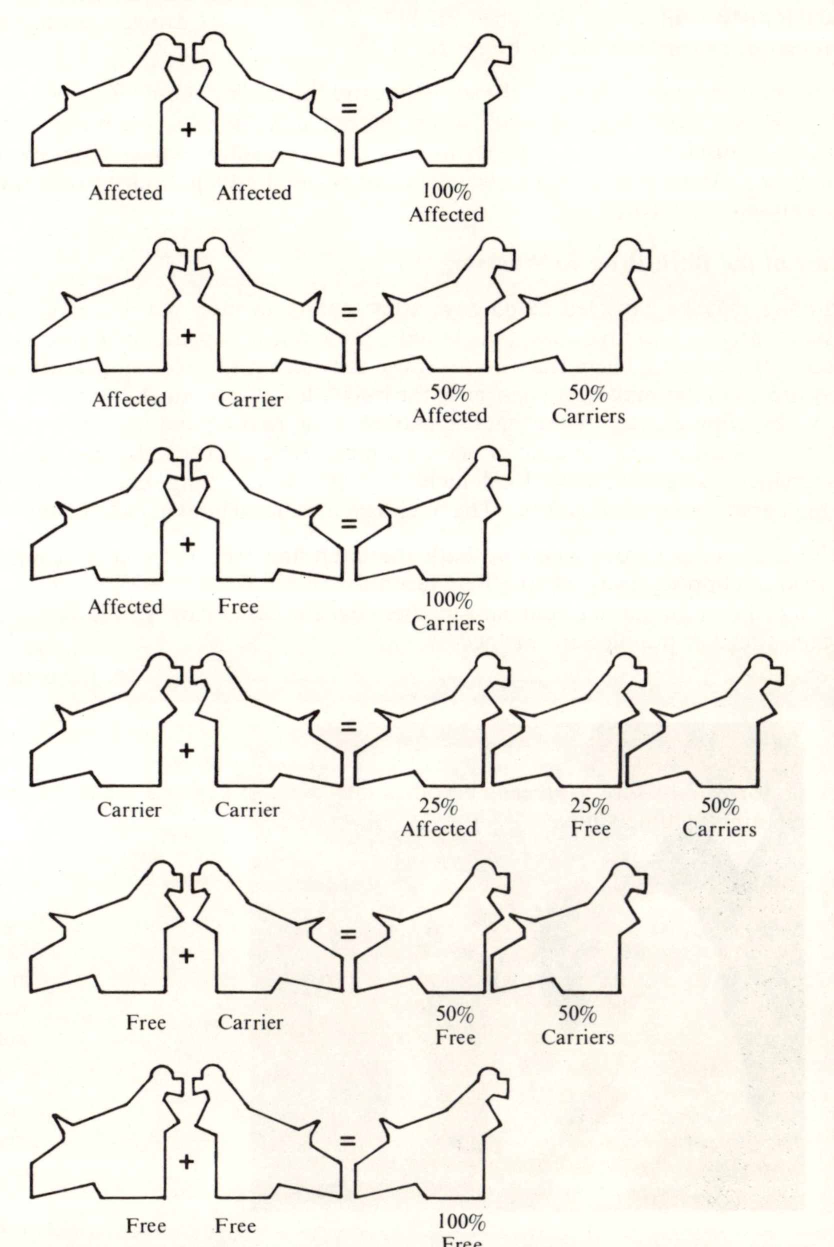
INHERITANCE OF CONDITIONS GOVERNED BY RECESSIVE GENES
eg. Hereditary Cataract, or Desired Colors
+
=
Affected
Affected
100%
Affected
Affected
Carrier
50%
Affected
50%
Carriers
Affected
Free
100%
Carriers
Carrier
Carrier
25%
Affected
25%
Free
50%
Carriers
Free
Carrier
50%
Free
50%
Carriers
Free
Free
100%
Free

Mating

The female is usually ready for mating between the 10th and 14th days of her cycle, but this is only a generalization. She may indicate her readiness to mate by switching her tail to one side when her back is stroked, by flirting, and when her vaginal discharge has lost its bright red color.

It is usual to take the bitch to the stud dog, and the mating should be supervised. Puppies are most likely to result when there is a tie, that is, when the bitch's internal muscles grip the dog's penis and the two cannot separate for several minutes — though puppies can be conceived without a tie provided the dog has penetrated the bitch.

Care of the Bitch Prior to Whelping

Puppies may be expected 59-63 days after mating. A litter which arrives early usually presents no problems, but should a bitch not whelp after 64 days consult your veterinarian. There may be no cause for alarm but professional advice is required. Do not make any changes in the bitch's lifestyle or nutrition for the first 5 weeks of pregnancy. After that she may want more food and it is advisable to offer it 3-4 times a day instead of one large meal. Do not over feed a bitch during pregnancy; use good quality food, including eggs, meat, cottage cheese, milk and a high grade commercial kibble. The bitch's greatest food intake is while lactating.

About 2 weeks before whelping bath the bitch and trim her coat as short as possible, clipping away all the hair around her nipples. Puppies can become strangled in a long, thick coat; shorten her coat for easier care. It will soon grow again after her puppies are weaned.

Note the beautiful 'plushy' look of these silver buff babies

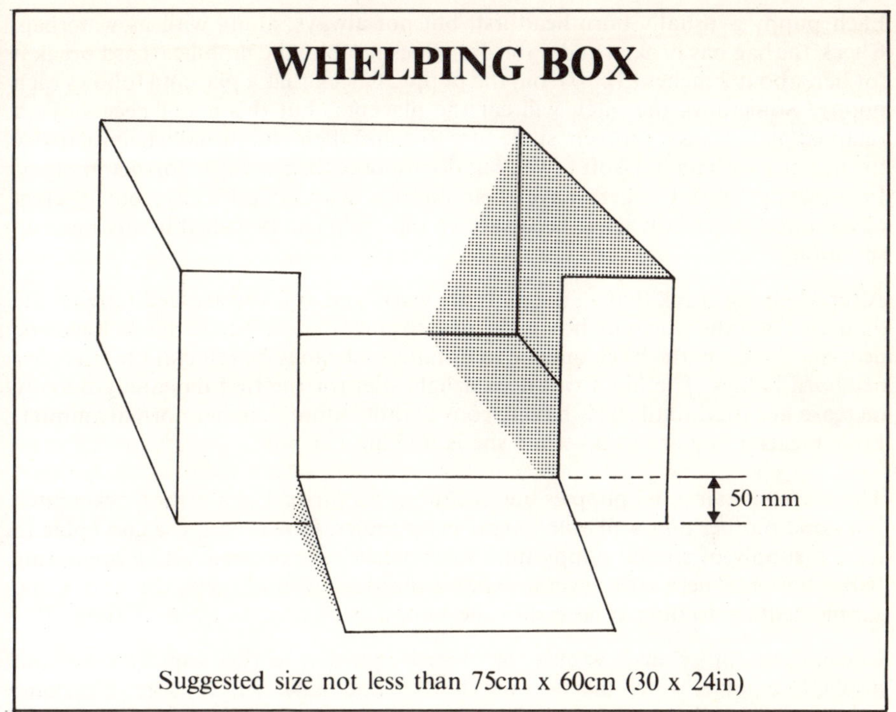

Suggested size not less than 75cm x 60cm (30 x 24in)

Whelping

A bitch needs to get used to her whelping quarters well before her pups are due. There are various types of whelping beds available, or one can be made at home either from wood or a heavy duty carton. A suggested size for a Cocker bitch is approximately 75 x 60 cm (30 x 24 in).

Privacy is also needed at whelping time and extra warmth, depending on the climate of course. A background heat of about 27°C (80°F) is necessary for the first few days as initially puppies cannot control their body heat. The temperature in the whelping area can gradually be reduced to normal room heat after about a week. Have stacks of newspapers ready and line the whelping box with single sheets of paper which can easily be changed as the whelping proceeds. Soiled papers should be placed in a garbage sack ready for disposal.

The Birth

When the birth is imminent the bitch's temperature drops from the normal 38.6°C (101.5°F) to about 37°C (99°F). At this time do not leave your bitch. See that she is in her whelping quarters but do not transfer any of your anxiety to her. Be prepared for the waiting vigil. The bitch's restlessness, the first stage of labor, gives way to straining and at this point watch the clock too. A bitch which is straining with no results after 2 hours needs veterinary help. Do not hesitate to get it.

Each puppy is usually born headfirst, but not always, along with its waterbag. Check the bag has broken and if the dam does not bite the umbilicalcord break it for her, about 2 inches (5 cm) from the puppy. Check that a placenta follows each puppy. Sometimes the bitch will eat the placenta, but this is not necessary. A retained placenta is a problem so be sure to count them. It is usually helpful to dry the puppies with an old, soft towel, but do not take them away from their mother. Fortunately most Cockers have their puppies without difficulty, but discreet observation by the owner is necessary so that help can be called in any unusual situation.

After whelping check that all the pups are warm and dry, and are feeding from the dam. See that the whelping box is cleaned up and offer the bitch a drink. It may be necessary to carry the bitch outside to urinate as she may be reluctant to leave her newborn babies. The bitch will need a light diet for the first day and gradually increase her food until she is having considerably more than her normal amount. Four meals a day are usual while she is nursing her pups.

The average litter is 4-7 puppies but of course this varies. Usually the Cocker bitch is a good mother and well able to rear her puppies. However, it is a good plan to have a supply of special puppy milk on hand in case of need, and a premature baby bottle. There are several reliable brands of milk replacer and if no supplementary feeding is necessary the milk can be used at weaning time.

Check the puppies' nails weekly, or more frequently, as they rapidly grow into needle-like points which may scratch the dam and make her very sore. The sharp points of the nails can be cut with ordinary nail scissors.

It is a good plan to apply early for the puppies' Kennel Club registration certificates so that they will be available when the puppies are ready to be sold.

Weaning

The puppies eyes open at about 12-14 days and weaning may commence at about 3 weeks. This is also the time to begin worming the pups using a preparation obtained from your veterinarian.

The pups first meal may either be some puppy milk mixed with baby cereal, a tiny taste of very fine ground beef, or a little commercially prepared puppy chow, depending on which way you intend to raise the litter. Many breeders consider variety is a fine thing; others rely solely on a commercial puppy diet which, when used as directed, is excellent. As weaning progresses the pups will need 4 meals a day, as much food as they can clear up in a reasonable time; at the same time decrease the dam's diet as her milk dries up. By the age of 6 weeks the pups should be fully weaned.

Vitamins

Commercially manufactured dog foods and puppy foods are already supplemented with vitamins and minerals and there is no need for the breeder to add more. If the pups have been weaned on to a plain meat and biscuit diet a complete vitamin/mineral additive may be used according to the manufacturer's directions. Do remember that an excess of vitamins can be as harmful as too little — if at all in doubt consult your veterinarian.

Veterinary Considerations

At the age of 4 days the puppies dew claws, which may be present on all four feet, should be removed, and the tails docked. This is not a job for the beginner so arrange for your veterinarian to call. The point at which the tail should be cut is just where it begins to taper. Avoid docking the tail too short.

Selling Puppies

Hopefully, the puppies registration certificates will be ready to give to their new owners. A comprehensive diet sheet should be prepared for each puppy, and a small supply of its usual food should be given to the purchaser so that no sudden change is made to its diet.

Be sure to keep proper records of sales as this saves time and worry in case any queries arise. Of course, you will have done your best to raise typical, healthy Cocker puppies, but remember that no guarantees can be given because how a puppy develops depends not only on your care but on its genetic background — some of which may be unknown to you — and the way its new owners rear it. Environment plays a vital part too.

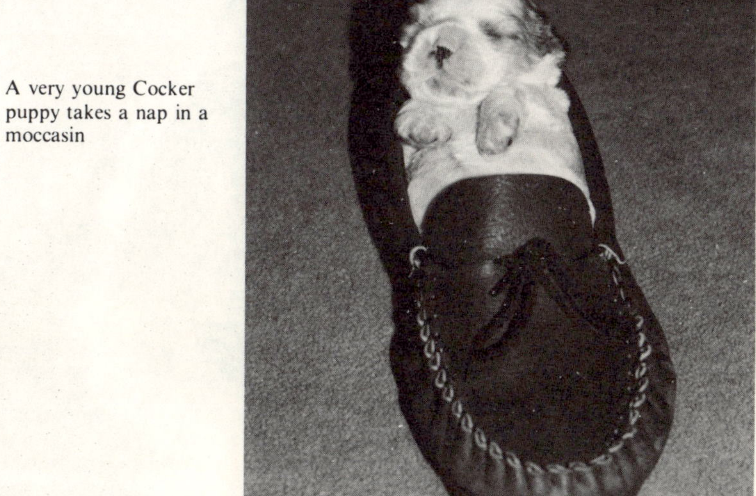

A very young Cocker puppy takes a nap in a moccasin

This Black Cocker is a British Show Champion

Particolor Cocker Spaniel

Suggested Further Reading

Grossman, A.	1977 — *Breeding Better Cocker Spaniels,* Denlinger, Fairfax, VA 22030
Harmar, H.	1968 — *Dogs and How to Breed Them,* John Gifford, London
	1969 — *Cocker Spaniel Guide,* Pet Library, New York
Kraeuchi, R.M.	1979 — *The New Cocker Spaniel,* Howell, New York

Gold and white Cocker Spaniel

Kennel Club Addresses

American Kennel Club
51 Madison Avenue
New York
N.Y. 10010, USA

Australian Kennel Club
Royal Show Grounds
Ascot Vale
Victoria
Australia

The Kennel Club
1 Clarges Street
Piccadilly
London, W.1.
England

Barbados Kennel Club
Wraysbury
Bucks, St Thomas
Barbados
West Indies

Bermuda Kennel Club Inc.
PO Box 1455
Hamilton 5
Bermuda

Canadian Kennel Club,
2150 Bloor Street West
Toronto M6S 1M8
Ontario
Canada

Kennel Club of India
Kenhope, Coonoor 1
Nilgiris
S. India

Irish Kennel Club
23 Earlsfort Terrace
Dublin 2
Eire

Jamaican Kennel Club
8 Orchard Street
Kingston 5
Jamaica
West Indies

Malaysian Kennel Association
PO Box 559
Kuala Lumpur
Malaya

Malta Kennel Club
1 Simon Flats
Dr Zammit Street
Balzan
Malta GC

New Zealand Kennel Club
PO Box 19
101 Aro Street
Wellington
New Zealand

The Singapore Kennel Club
275f Selegie Complex
Selegie Road
Singapore 7

Kennel Union of Southern Africa
6th Floor, Bree Castle
68 Bree Street
Cape Town 8001
South Africa